BIRDS THAT LIVE IN THE NORTH

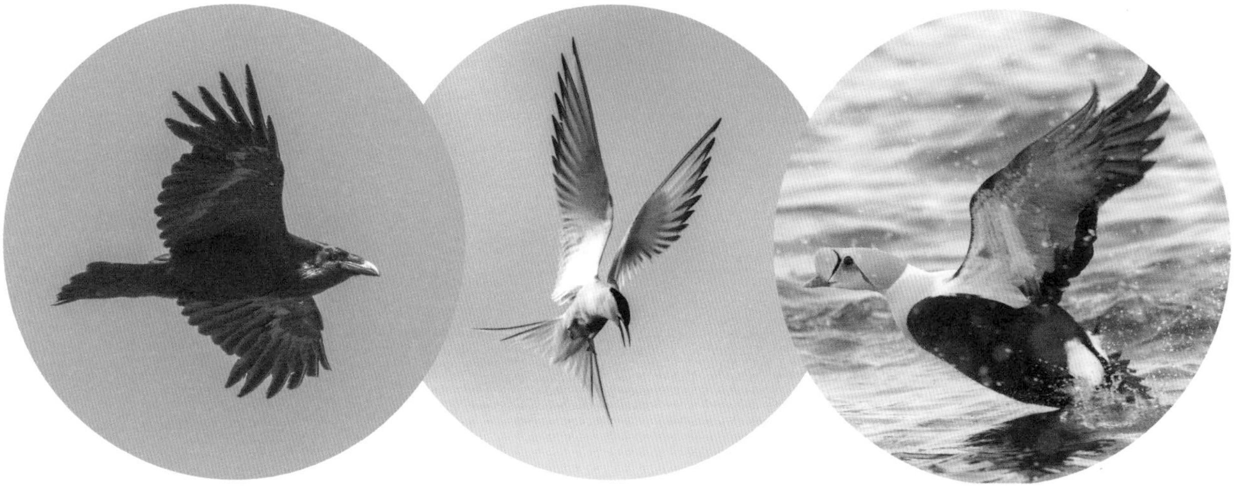

raven

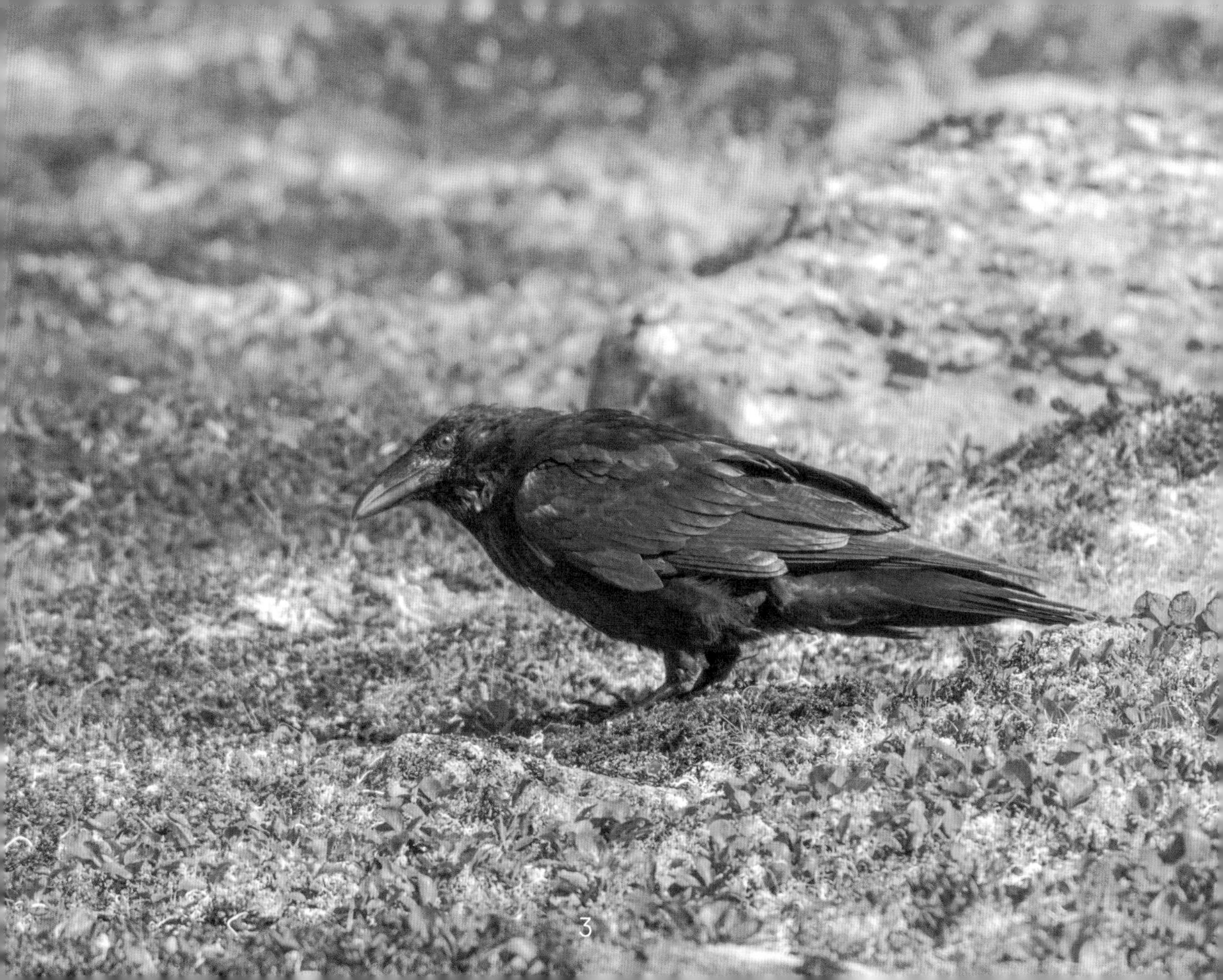

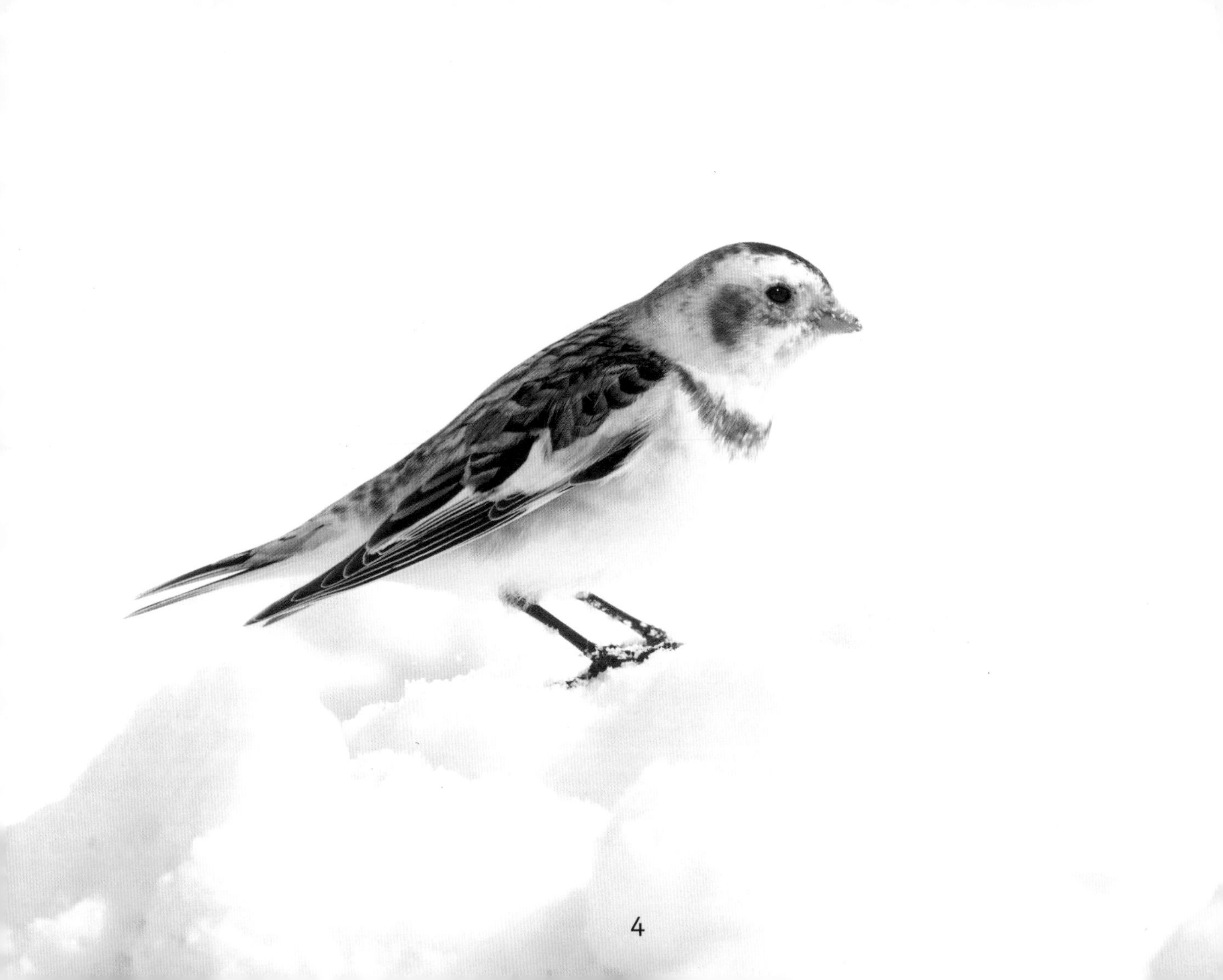

snow bunting

Arctic tern

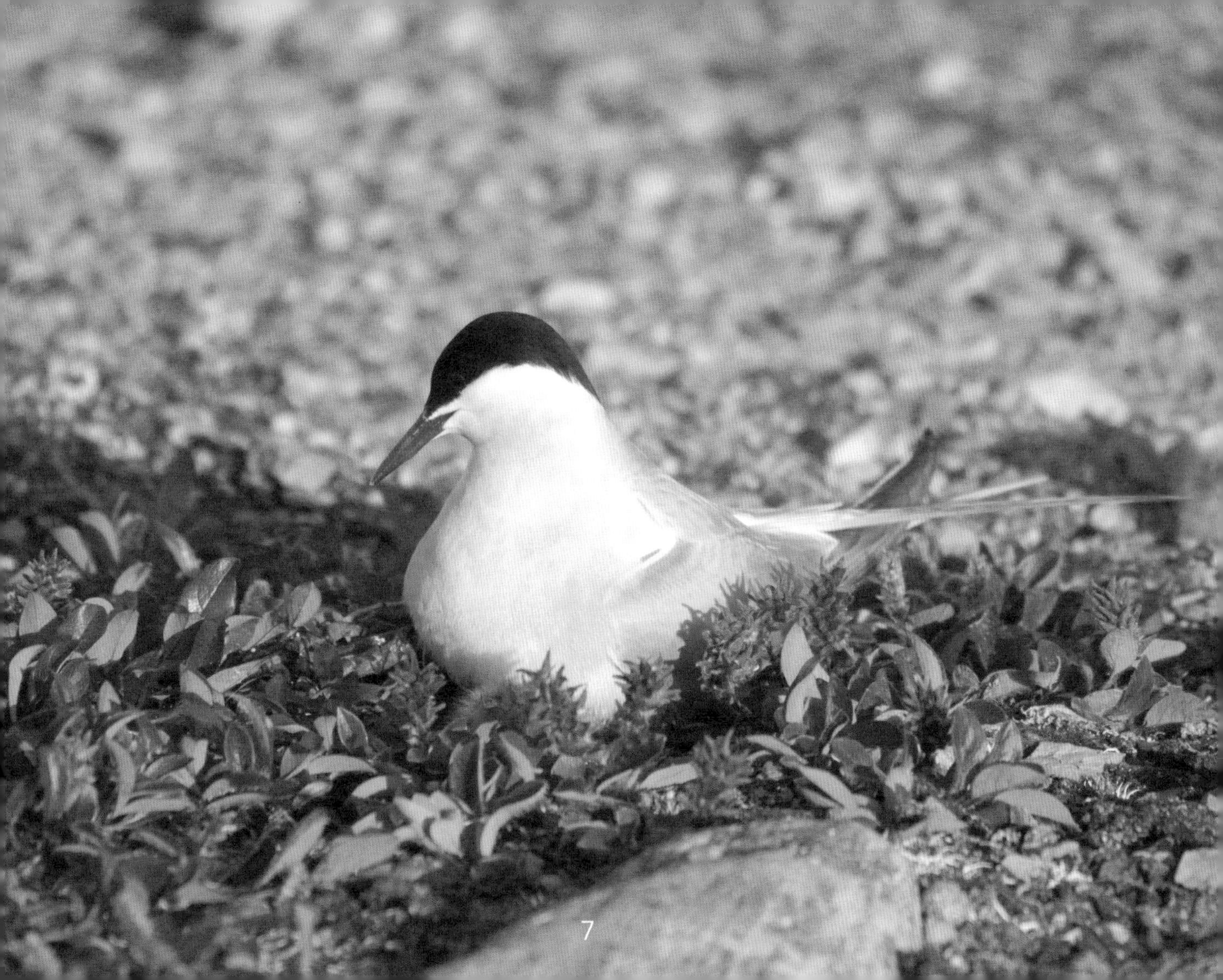

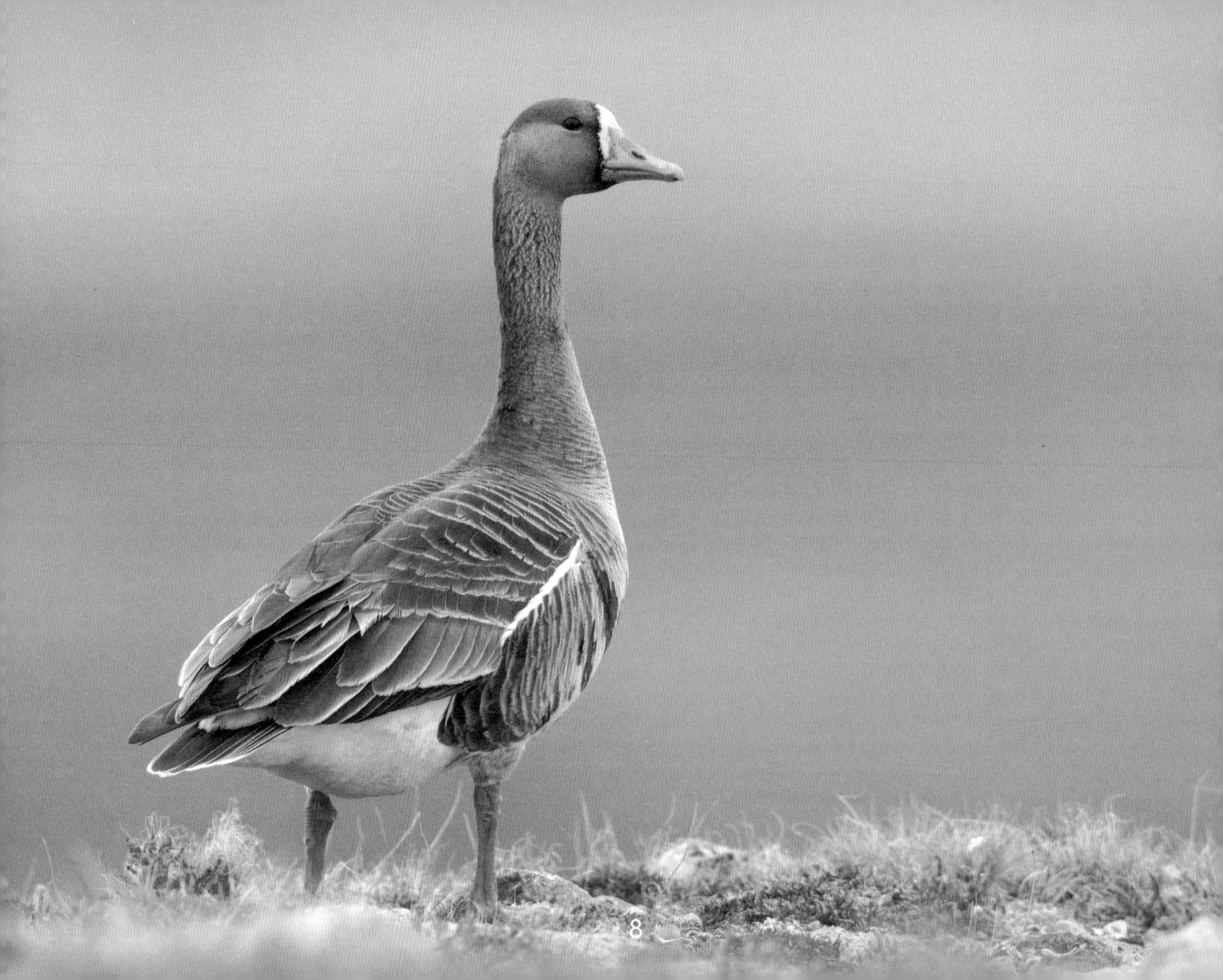

goose

duck

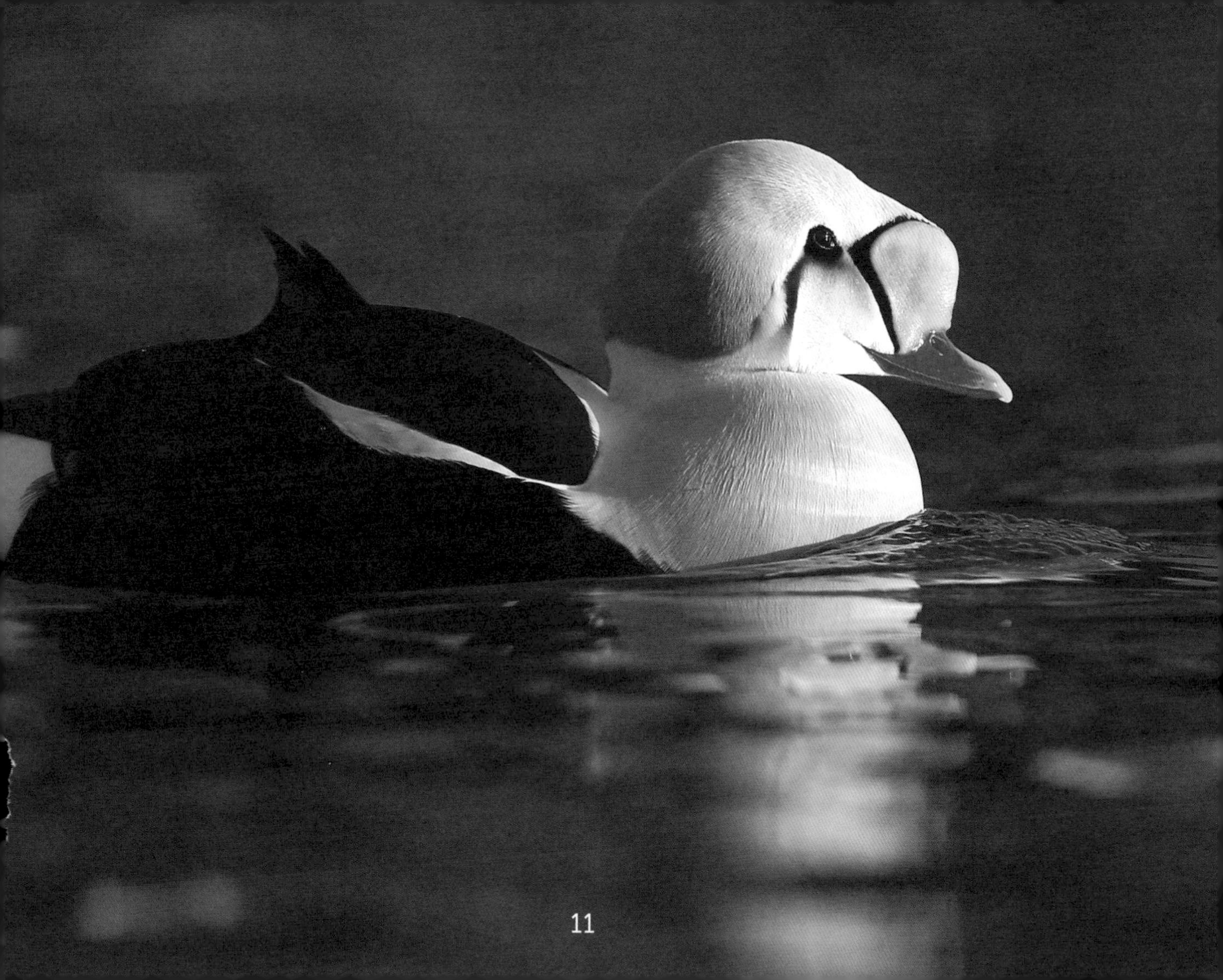

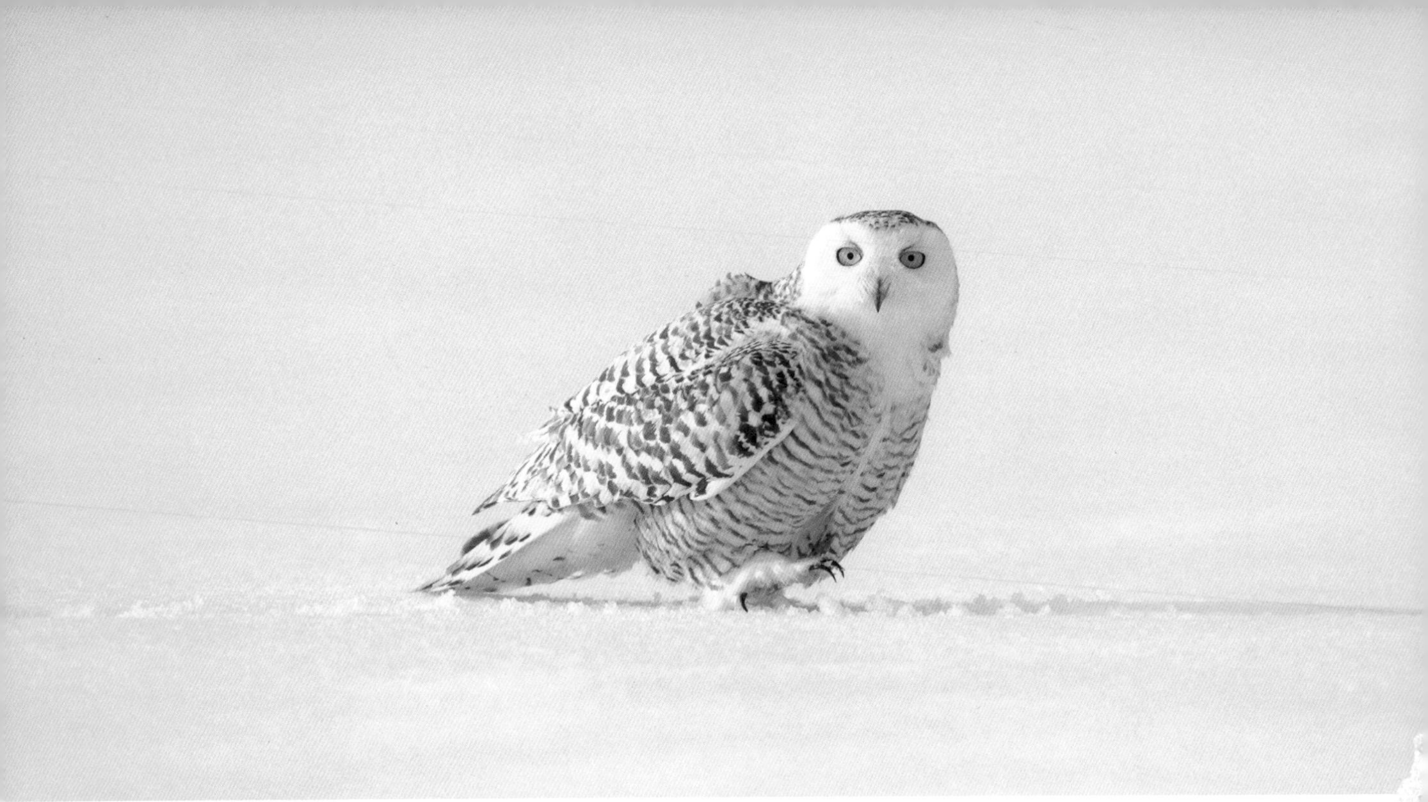

owl